Born on Lake Shuswap

Memories and Thoughts

Born on Lake Shuswap
Memories and Thoughts

Joan Vernon Szabo

3Sister
PRESS

Copyright © 2024 by 3SisterPress. All rights reserved. No part of this publication may be reproduced, distributed, or transmitted in any form or by any means, including photocopying, recording, or other electronic or mechanical methods, without the prior written permission of the publisher, except in the case of brief quotations embodied in critical reviews and certain other noncommercial uses permitted by copyright law. For permission requests, write to
    MartaSzabo@AuthenticWriting.com.
and its logos are copyright © 2024 of 3SisterPress.
    108 Tinker Street
    Woodstock NY 12498
Ordering Information:
    For details, contact: MartaSzabo@AuthenticWriting.com
Print ISBN: 9780996412230
Printed in the United States of America
    First Edition
Design, production, editing, and illustration credits:
    Book design and production: small packages, inc
        smallpackages.com
    Front Cover Image: Joan Vernon Szabo, circa 1940
    Back Cover Image: Miklos Szabo-Pelsoczi, circa 1955

DEDICATION

We dedicate this book to our Canadian family — past, present and future.
Our grandparents:
    Herman (Pops) Vernon 1884 - 1960
    Augusta (Mopsie) Vernon 1899 - 1991

Our mother and her siblings:
    Edwin (Ed) 1918 - 1990
    Elizabeth (Bets) 1919 - 2019
    Sylvia (Muña / Moon) 1921 - 1987
    Joan (Gin) 1924 - 2020
    Mary (Pear, spelled Pr) 1925 - 2017
    Richard (Dick) 1927 - 2017
    Phyllis (Billy) 1932 - 2005

We also dedicate this to our cousins who remember hearing the stories of those early years…and to their children and grandchildren who carry the spirit of the stories in their bones.

And to Lake Shuswap which stayed alive in our mother's heart long after she left the area.

We hope you enjoy these unpretentious expressions from a woman who was never one to blow her own trumpet.

We will be forever grateful to have had her as our "Mum."

~ Marta, Anasuya and Kanaka

Contents

Shuswap Lake	1
Our Childhood Home	4
My Parents	8
Pi	11
My Mother	14
My Father	16
Sheep	19
The Sorrento Store and Our Gardens	22
My Father: The Warts	26
Myself	28
Edwin	31
Muña	35
School	38
My Best Teacher	40
The Neighbors at Sorrento	42
The Characters of My Childhood	46
Flowers from My Childhood	48
Teen Age	50
Making Hay	54
Mountaineering on the Elephant's Toes	57
Migration	59
Going to Vancouver	61

Picking Fruit	64
In Montreal	66
My Good Friend	69
After University Ends	71
Settling Down	74
1200 Park Avenue and I	76
About Aging	78
Waiting for the Bus	80
Things We Can Do to Cheer Up Our World	82
An Afternoon Walk	83
Is There Hope for Us?	85
Beauty	88
Forest Ranch	90
Reflections	92
AFTERWORD—Return to Sorrento	95

This book has an online photo gallery.

Please visit: http://AuthenticWriting.com/Shuswap

Shuswap Lake

Sorrento, where I spent my childhood, was situated on the land sloping up from Shuswap Lake. "Shuswap" is an Indian word meaning "shimmering waters." The lake was over 30 miles long and had two arms reaching far into the interior. At Sorrento it was two to three miles wide. From our side we looked across to wooded mountains stretching to the East and as far as the Selkirk mountains.

There was a ferry that chugged across on the hour. It took about 15 minutes, and on the next hour it chugged back. The ferry captain was an important man in the community. He took his job very seriously and the ferry was always on time. It was a connection to the villages on the other side. One family on the other side sent their three boys to our school, so they had a long day, coming on the first ferry at 8am, and going home on the five o'clock from our side.

Our family didn't own any lakeside property; we lived about a mile above. But we always went to a special area and kept our boat and picnic table there. We called it "our beach."

We worked at home on summer mornings, and the younger

ones could go to the lake in the afternoon, as long as at least a 12-year-old sibling went to watch them swimming. Those were lovely days. We picked ripe berries on the way down and back. The water was cooling and cleansing.

On Sundays my mother would make potato salad, hard boiled eggs and rolls, and lemonade, so we would take a picnic. It was special because our mother came too and went swimming with us. Sometimes we went out in the rowboat trolling for trout. They bit better in the early morning, but once in a while we caught a fish in the afternoon or early evening.

During August for a few weeks my mother and several of us would camp for a week or so at the lake. The men brought down a big tent, bedrolls, food and necessary utensils in the wagon. They set up the tent and got my mother settled. She always brought a nice mattress because she never wanted to sleep on hard ground.

I learned to arrange the boughs of a fir tree so the big stems were tucked under the previously laid row – when finished it would be springy. Over that, I laid my bedding. It was fun to sleep in the open and look up at the sky at night. In the early morning I could hear the loon way out in the lake calling his lonely yodel and perhaps his mate would answer it.

My father sometimes came for a swim in the evenings. The older teenagers did the cooking at the farm because work and animals don't take vacations. Even some of us at the lake had to go up and bring the cows from pasture at five o'clock for the milking. It was still a fine thing to be camping. I have loved it ever since then.

As we got older, in our teens, camping at the lake got tame – so we did other things like bonfires at night, with corn, or hotdogs. All the local young people came and some brought guitars and we sang. Couples would steal away into the woods. Some of us went swimming at night. It seemed quite exciting in the dark. By the time I became a teenager, the lake didn't freeze over in the winter, but I remember as a little girl that it did. The memory of my older sisters pushing me along as I tried to keep up on wobbly ankles trying to skate is uncomforting.

All in all, the lake was a big part of our lives – a great treasure. A few miles West the lake narrowed into the Little River, which flowed into the Thompson River on its 350-mile journey down to Vancouver and the Pacific Ocean.

Our Childhood Home

Our house in Sorrento was built in 1923. It is still in good shape at 91 years old and has been inhabited constantly, after my father sold it in 1952. It was built in the Dutch Colonial style on two floors, no attic to speak of, and no basement. Four dormer windows faced the East and one faced West – and the sunset. The windows were all casement-type, opening out like doors, with little panes.

The front door faced East and was only used for guests. As family and neighbors, we all used the back door; it faced South and its porch was attached to the garage/woodshed. This door led into a small wood room where the split pieces were stored for the kitchen cook-stove. There was a shelf for the kerosene can; we called it coal oil and used it for lamps. This room led into the washroom, also small like today's mudroom, with a washing machine powered by water, and a big deep sink.

From there you entered the kitchen. It was a big square room with windows facing East and South, so it was usually bright. I think of it as yellow because my mother liked yellow curtains and cream-colored walls. Against one side was the stove and it was called the black bastard if my mother was angry at it because it wouldn't get hot quickly when she needed to cook bread or pies. On another wall was the kitchen sink with shelves on either side, with pots and pans below, and dishes in a rack over the sink so they dripped into the sink while drying. I saw one or two dish racks like this in English houses, but not in Canada. The cutlery we dried by hand, a chore we did three times a day since we were a big family and would not otherwise have had enough for the next meal.

On the West wall of the kitchen and parallel to it was the long table, and it would seat eight. The smaller children sat on a built-in banco (or bench) on the window side, the big ones opposite, and the parents at each end. Usually there was a hired man too, and the older girl or two would sit at a tall table against the South windows. So there was always room for an extra friend or help. From the kitchen you went into the playroom. Against the West window was another built-in banco. When you opened the lid it was full of toys, often quite battered. To the left was a couch or a single bed where my younger brother slept after he left the girls room at age seven.

There was a big furnace meant to heat the upstairs. We had running water in the kitchen, bathroom and in the adult bedrooms upstairs, and in zero weather the pipes would freeze if the heat wasn't kept on 24/7. Big pieces of wood, and at night coal, would keep the temperature above freezing, if not warm. There was a bathroom off the playroom and a hall leading to the front door, the living room, and on the other side to the stairs.

The living room was on the North side and occupied the full width of the house. There were windows on the North, West and East. The curtains were deep blue. There was a black shiny table, two big easy chairs in front of the fireplace, and shelves of books. On the Northeast side stood an upright piano, also black and shiny, rather grand; at first my father would play but his hands got coarse with farmer's work so he would play the pianola. This way, he put rolls in a slot in the piano front and pumped the pedals and the music would come out clear and beautiful, like magic.

Upstairs was reached from the hall. The staircase was enclosed, and the landing at the top was a warm space if the upstairs door was shut, and we dressed there on cold mornings. Cozy. The second storey began in the middle of the house, in a hall with the only dormer window facing West. That window witnessed occasional crashing of birds. They were blinded by the setting sun and flew right into it and died.

There was a passage from the hall the length of the house joining my parents' rooms – my mother's on the South, my father's on the North. My mother's room seemed cozy and bright, and big. It had a door leading to the "kids' room." This is where Dick, Mary and I shared two beds, Dick in a narrow one and Mary and I in a big one. I remember we both ended up in the middle all the time because the mattress sagged. That room and each of the other three bedrooms had a window facing East.

On the North side of the central hall were two bedrooms. The big one was my father's. I slept there in a cot before I was seven, and moved to the "kids' room." The other bedroom was smaller and opened onto the top landing of the stairs. First it belonged to my oldest brother Edwin, then when he decided he was too grown up for the "other kids" he moved into the shack where he shared two rooms with the hired man. Here he was a man. Then Bets first and Muña second got Ed's room and when they had left home, I got to have it to myself – great feeling.

This about sums up the whole house – it was not insulated the way houses are today and heat was not steady. Sometimes the pipes froze in zero weather. I don't remember pipes bursting ever. We always managed to unfreeze them with hot water. In the summer, it was a great addition to have screens, for the flies were all around and the windows open for the fresh air.

My Parents

I can't talk about my childhood without first mentioning my parents. An odd couple - totally opposite. First, my father. He was a businessman turned farmer. He was intellectual, self-taught, had lived in Europe, South America and now in British Columbia. He was a married man with a total of seven children, but in his heart a bachelor. My mother was from Uruguay, spoke English second, after Spanish. She married my father when she was 18, my father, 34. They moved from Uruguay to England, my father's country.

My mother thought England damp, cold, and unfriendly. My father thought it was too crowded. He had retired from business and wanted to try farming. Brochures from Canada, the Pacific, welcomed all to come! And so my parents, by then laden with three children, took a boat to Montreal, a train to British Columbia, and settled on 160 acres of virgin woods and open land.

My mother told us much later that during the first very cold winter they spent in a log cabin where you had to chop wood and haul water, she felt she would go crazy. She was going to leave and take the children back to her country. But when April came, the snow melted. All kinds of birds came back. She loved the songbirds — because of them she stayed.

By the summer, my father had the house ready enough to move in. There was running water, piped by gravity from a spring higher up on the land. An indoor toilet, and a wood stove, for sure. But also an oven and a big surface. So my mother got some relief. It was a good thing because the following spring, the fourth child, me, was born at home.

My mother loved children, especially newborns. She said that ever since she was a little girl she would ask everyone to mind their babies, so if she ended up with seven that was fine with her. If my mother went away for a day, I was forlorn. The house was not fine. My father didn't offer too much. He kept telling us to be quiet, that we were noisy, wretched children. From his point of view he was right. So we learned to avoid him, together and/or alone, depending on the situation. When he was inside, we stayed outside. There were good playing places. He let us have a pony. Often, we tagged along with the hired man, got trips on his wagon — into the fields and into the woods, where he cut wood.

We had chores, more or less, according to our ages. We had to do those chores properly or we'd encounter my father's wrath. That was very scary. We got paid once a month, and that was a good thing to keep us from forgetting responsibility. As we got older, we had to help milk the cows morning and evening. As children we were good at it. Our fingers were smooth and supple. We were gentler than the men, and the animals trusted us. We never hit them in anger, as the men did. By then, my father had a good team of support. He himself was no good with the cows. He fed them and cleaned the gutters, and did those chores.

Both my brothers were good with animals. They were also handy with machinery and carpentry. The girls were good in the house and garden and taking care of the cows, sheep and chickens. Work on a farm was endless, but we had the lake, about a mile away, all downhill. In the summer we could swim there afternoons and evenings. We had a rowboat too, and fished sometimes — for trout.

There were many good times in my childhood, and some bad times. Our family could be called dysfunctional by today's standards. My parents fought often, or didn't speak to one another. I felt caught between. I loved my mother. I was pretty scared of my father, but I needed to stick up for him. He found books for me. I read Robinson Crusoe, Treasure Island, Jane Eyre, and many others. Books were my escape.

Pi

Pi was our family dog when I was growing up. When I was five, he was a pup. His mother was a collie-type dog called Lassie. She had a bad habit of chasing cars, and one day a car hit her and injured her so she had to be put to sleep. So Pi grew up alone as the other pups were given away.

My father called him Rover. How we started to call him Pi, I don't know. When asked why, we said it was because he was 22.7 purebred! Actually, he had a mixture of colors, brown, black and white. His hair was long and wavy, and we would clip it around his eyes so he could see better. He lived outside mostly. He had a bed under the back porch.

Nobody could come to the house without him barking fiercely. We had to hold him sometimes because he especially barked at the Indian women when they came around to trade baskets, beaded leather gloves and vests, for potatoes, apples and canned fruits. They were terrified of Pi. We had one neighbor, not being good with animals, who had kicked Pi as a puppy. That dog never forgot, and when the neighbor came around we had to tie up the growling beast. But in general, apart from doing his job as a watchdog, Pi was a pretty gentle, friendly soul.

He came with me the first time I went to school. I followed the white tip of his tail as he led me through the trail that we took to get there. I came home early, before the bigger kids, and he was there to bring me home. He went everywhere on our family picnics, walks, errands, when we delivered milk, or went to the store or post office.

Since it always involved walking, we were happy to have him along, especially at night going through the trails, which were our way of travel. He would go ahead and we could see the tip of his tail — white in the dark. I found it reassuring because he would take care of bears or tigers, which might otherwise pounce on me in the dark.

Pi came with us when we took the sheep out to the pasture. We had to herd them a short distance along the main road. Cars would stop. People would admire our handsome dog. They sometimes said he was like the English sheepdog. To be truthful, he was not good at herding sheep; he would run if an angry ewe turned to confront him. Our brave little hero!

Pi subsisted on oatmeal porridge and milk, and the occasional bone all his life. He was known to raid the neighbor's garbage can. Many a time I saw him happily bringing home a ham bone which he would gnaw at for hours.

In spite of this, Pi lived to be 18 years old. He was pretty blind the last year or two, and he was allowed to live in the kitchen where it was always warm in the winter.

Even up to the end, he had a happy spirit, and if he could he would have lived on for years. His life was free and he wandered where he wanted. Perhaps simple things were what kept him going so long.

My Mother

My mother was born in 1899 in Fray Bentos, Uruguay. She was the youngest in a family of eight children. Her mother and father had come from Germany and Austria; they had met as teenagers on the boat coming over. I never met my grandparents.

She was raised in an easy-going and probably happy family. She told us that when one in the family was sick, an old woman with a big stick would come in and circle the patient a few times. She would bang on the floor repeatedly with her stick and then leave. I don't know if her mother believed it would help. My mother would laugh as she told us.

In 1918 my mother met my father who had a big job as manager of an English company and got married. He was 16 years older and quite a loner and intellectual. My mother was a good-natured girl, sturdy, and not intellectual at all. I never thought of her as a loner.

After they were married, they had two children in Uruguay. Another baby was born in England. My father was English but neither of my parents liked living there much, so they came to Canada.

The first winter was very hard. They were living in a cabin

and my father hadn't even learnt to split wood for the stoves. So it was only in the spring that my mother began to enjoy the woods and fields of British Columbia. She liked the birds singing and the wildflowers everywhere.

My father had a nice house built in the early 1920s. It had a real bathroom and running water in the kitchen, bathroom and laundry room. They had a big stove for cooking, a furnace to keep the rest of the house warm in the winter and bedrooms for the children and the parents. My mother felt better there.

As the 1920s came to a close, they had six children, four girls and two boys. The Depression was a hard time, especially for my father.

My Father

My father was born in England in 1884, the age of Queen Victoria. It was a good time to be English then because good jobs could be had in most places in the world. He grew up in a middle class family and had to go to work at age 14. This was not unusual in those days. He worked as an office boy. It was at the time when phones were starting to be used. He said they terrified him. No one showed him how to answer a phone, so he would simply shout, "I'm sorry, I don't know how!" without lifting the receiver.

He learned German, French and Spanish at night school. And when he was 19 he went to Germany to teach English. After a few years he went to Uruguay to become the secretary to the boss of a meat packing company and he stayed there until he became the boss. There he married my mother and had two children.

He retired and they went to England. My mother didn't like England much. My father thought he would buy a farm. He was sick of business and wanted the peace and quiet of country life. They had three children now. They decided to move to British Columbia, Canada. There they bought a piece of new virgin farmland and built a house and settled down.

My father wasn't so good at ordinary farm work. He was clumsy but persistent. The local Canadians laughed at his efforts but it didn't affect him much. He had a hired man who could do field work, also mechanical things. He must have thought it a blessing when my older brother finished grade school and worked with the hired men and learned quickly to build and take care of machinery, all the many practical talents required for farming.

My father did all the chores, feeding the cows and the bulls, the pigs, and separating the milk. He did his share of work, but all his spare time he read. He kept up with philosophy and new learning.

In the meantime, we were seven noisy children and sometimes a big trial. He would say we were a wretched lot and leave it all to my mother. She, on the other hand, had a good time with us and we loved her.

Although we knew everyone in our tiny district, my father kept to himself. When they opened a little branch library, he would go and borrow books. Sometimes my sister or myself would take one of the afternoon library shifts. He scarcely recognized us. Then he might say, "By jove! It's Joan!" as if I weren't there. He was so absent minded. Parties, he hated. Once he stayed in his bedroom while we gave a party. Everyone in the area came, it was something to do. In those days no one had TV and radio wasn't too good.

One older man went to spend time at the party with my father in his bedroom. The next day my dad said that the man was an "ass." He spent his time saying that his life was hard, and "what was it all about anyway?" My dad advised him to enjoy it as well as he could, and it was the only one we had.

We got, it turns out, a good training in hard and persistent work, and being prudent with money. In these general things my dad was good. But he remained at heart a bachelor and a loner.

When he reached 65, the Canadian government sent him his first monthly payment of the old age pension. This is done for everyone, unsolicited. My dad was overcome with surprise and spent time wondering if he should accept. No one had ever, in all his life, given him free money. Finally, he decided that because he had always paid his bills and taxes on time, that he would accept. In the end he must have found it a blessing.

Sheep

When I was quite little, until my middle teens, we had a flock of sheep on our farm, about 70 to 80 of them — enough anyway to make a solid group that made cars stop while we had to cross the highway to get to the fields. The highway cut through our farm.

March and April was the lambing season. Sometimes the ewes needed help, and occasionally an ewe would die giving birth. Then we would feed the little lamb from a bottle, and take him into the warm kitchen where we made a box for them near the cookstove, which always gave warmth. Such a lamb grew up as a pet until it was big enough to fend for itself in the flock. As children, we loved the lambs, named our favorites, and spent a long time with them in the sheep pens.

In May the sheep shearer would come around and shear all the sheep. One by one he would grab a sheep, lay it on its side, and snip off the whole fleece starting at the neck and ending at the hind quarters. He was expert, and took off the whole fleece in one piece, then rolled it up and tied it with string. He worked all morning until he had done them all. Then he sat down to a plate of meat and vegetables my mother brought for him, and polished it off. He would leave, and go off to the next farm without saying very much at all.

After the shearing, the sheep were again caught one by one and dipped into a vat of water and tick-killing chemicals. Then they were left to nurse the lambs and enjoy their pasture. We shrimps (as we three young ones were called) were always watching at these important times, feeling sorry for the bald ewes.

Every year in early June the sheep were sent to the mountain high pastures for the summer. By then, the lambs were sturdy enough to make the strenuous journey. Early on, my father would take ours, but later my big brother took them. He was 15 and knew about camping and hiking. It was a big relief to my father.

They took Prince, our riding horse, as a pack horse, loaded with the camping gear, food and clothing for four or five days. Then off they'd go, driving our flock, followed by the neighbor behind him, to the ferry which took them all across the lake and onto seven miles along the highway to near the foot of the mountain trail. They stayed at a farm there and put all the sheep in a field with water, for it had been a long day.

The next morning they made it up the mountain. It was a long and at times steep climb, so it took pretty much all day. But the summit was beautiful and flat, and spread in all directions — lush with flowers and thick grass. A shepherd was there to take charge of all the sheep for the summer. After an overnight there, the men made the long trip back home, without sheep.

In early September, the trip was done again, in reverse, because by then the mountain would be getting cold and snow possible. We shrimps would wait for the sheeps' return. Then, as they came off the ferry, you could hear them baa-ing all the way up the winding hill. When they got close to home, they started to run and we opened the big gate to let them into the lane. The poor things were so happy to reach their old sheep-pen, and so were we. They were ready for hay and water, and a long rest.

The Sorrento Store and Our Gardens

Sorrento, BC — it is very natural, I find, to write that address. No zip code. 70 years ago. A small post office and general store.

We went to a wicket sort of window and the postman picked through and gave us the mail from our box behind there. It came every day from the train. A car made it to Notch Hill where the train stopped, either from Vancouver or coming from the East to the Coast. The postman doubled as a storekeeper and daily newspaper — they always knew the local gossip or news. It was a meeting place: men gathered around a register in the back — warm air coming up from a basement furnace, and stomped their feet in winter and rubbed their hands. They discussed the roads, the boxing championships and other manly fare. Women towed in children and did shopping.

Dogs remained on the outside and there were many good dog fights among enemies: our dog Pi didn't like Zipper the storekeeper's dog, or Mac, another dog who belonged to good friends. Sometimes a lot of dogs would get in a fight. Then the storekeeper would shake hot pepper over them to separate them. It worked fine. So for a few hours, not many, the centre of public life was "the store." It was very important to us.

As kids, we were sent down with letters to post, stamps to buy, money orders to get, and mail and the newspaper to bring home. Sometimes we bought cheese which they cut from a big wheel in the back, sometimes bread if we were short. The bread was terrible, "all air" we used to say, and "you couldn't fill up on it." The farmer's wife had to "fill up" a lot of hungry stomachs three times a day, so homemade bread was heavier and solid. Also less expensive.

These times were the 30's — no one had extra money, but no one in our community went hungry. At least, I don't think so. When a family was down on their luck, others chipped in with clothes, vegetables, and dairy products. If people were able bodied they could grow enough to eat. The land was good, a sort of clay and black loam. But you had to work it hard and regularly and that way you got results.

Even as small kids we all liked gardens. I had a little piece about six feet square and I put stones all round it and a big stone on one side I could sit on. We would ask Mopsie for a plant or two, and sometimes put in our own seeds. I had a flag (iris), lots of pansies, some little daisies, a sweet william and so on. Pr had a longer and narrower garden, and she had her own plants. Dick had one in between ours. He had some flowers. But his best fun was making ditches and emptying buckets of water down them. In the summer his garden baked hard in the sun, but it didn't worry him. By the time we got gardens, Ed and Bets were big, entering their teens and weren't interested in their gardens. Moon kept hers for a time, and since she was a bit older hers always seemed rather a fine thing to me.

I would go every morning in spring and early summer to check if a flower came out, or if some seeds came up. Then I'd rush in with the news, not that anyone else really cared but for me it was what made the day! By late summer interest waned and I'd leave it til the next Spring.

The big garden around our house was planted originally with great care and thought. By the time I remember, around 1929 or 1930, there was a nice rose arbor on the West side, and paths led past beds with sweet williams or flag borders and shrubs of all sorts scattered throughout. The beds had brick borders. There were lilacs, mock orange, forsythia, spirea, quince, and other things with shasta daisies interspersed.

I remember my mother showing visitors through it so it must have looked nice. Later though it was hard to keep up. Shrubs got out of hand, and grass crept in and the perennials disappeared. In the later 30's, Mopsie fixed it up with new plants she got. She worked so hard on it, I remember her with sweat on her face digging away, but she liked to do that, and she brought home new plants from her friends' gardens.

The East side of the house faced the fields and a "bush" (woods). Beyond, there was grass in the middle, and on either side were walks bordered by beds of plants again. So there were lots of gardens to take care of. Mopsie put tulips and daffodils and crocuses there in front. Once in a while, maybe someone cut the grass with a push mower or even a scythe. There was a substantial hedge of white spirea against the field. In the middle of the grass I remember my father would sit on a white canvas deck chair and read. He always read. I remember him mostly as reading, pushing a wheelbarrow, or hollering at his pigs. He used to say that pigs and cows were smarter than horses and dogs, but he still hollered every day at them. He didn't bother much with the horses or dogs. Which was a blessing. He wasn't much good with animals. Fortunately, we all were good with animals so the less he did, the happier all around. But he kept his pigs and we didn't do much with them.

My Father: The Warts

Previously I wrote of my father, telling the things I remembered, recounting the more positive and pleasant aspects of his personality. However, I have other disquieting memories that are troubling me, and I know my sisters too.

My father was not a born farmer. It was an ideal he cherished while living in cities as a businessman. His attitude to animals was impersonal; they were regarded either as money-makers or as a nuisance. When he first tried to milk a cow, he approached it as a power struggle he needed to win. We children learnt to milk by first accepting that the cow was our friend, and between us we got the task done. My father meanwhile had to hogtie the cow, and even then she resisted letting down her milk from sheer fear and nervousness. Luckily for all, he gave over the milking to us children. The barn became a peaceful place.

The newborn calves were separated from their mothers immediately after birth. This is the way with dairy cows because they give more milk then. If my father had to train the calves to drink their milk from a pail, he was defeated again because he hit and kicked the calf until it was even more stupid.

I could teach a calf to drink by the second or third day. You put your fingers in their mouth and then dipped the head into the pail of warm milk. In a while they got the hang of it and the poor little beast became happy and satisfied. It was awful if my father tried it, he was cruel.

He was also sometimes mean to his pigs. He liked pigs, he said, but when he fed them they would assert their piggy habits of pushing and gobbling and putting their feet in the trough. If he was in a bad mood, he would take a pitchfork and stab the ones he thought were the worst. He would stand there and watch and then stab the ones that were more aggressive, even drawing blood.

I guess the poor animals were the whipping boys of his bad moods and lack of enjoyment in the work. It was a blessing when he sold the farm after we all grew up and left home. Then he had no big responsibilities for children and animals, and he could read more. His saving grace was the reading that he loved to do.

Myself

I have few memories before the age of five. But a lot of memories when my parents and older siblings talked about bushfires. I seemed to remember them too, but they said I couldn't remember as it happened years before when I was one or two. I still have those memories and I wonder whether the flames and smoke I saw looking out of the window was real. I'll never know for sure. Probably not.

All through school, there were four of us in our grade. I am still friends with one of us. Bunny is in a home now but is spry and still drives. I was a scrappy kid if anyone sassed me. I took care of myself and if I couldn't my older sister got into the scrap and sent my enemy running.

I read books avidly, at first adventure stories, then detective — like Agatha Christie and Sherlock Holmes. I still like mysteries and murders.

I used to collect bird feathers and bird eggs. It was said that if you only took one egg from a nest the bird would not notice. Hindsight tells me that wasn't true; the bird would smell an intruder and vacate the nest.

I visited my two friends, one of whom went nest hunting with me. We could go to each other's house for meals. I liked her house because they ate differently. And her mother called her father "darling." I wasn't used to hearing affectionate words either. My father either talked up a storm at meals or went for days absent minded and silent.

My sister and I belonged to Girl Guides, the Canadian version of the Girl Scouts. Our uniform was a navy blue dress with a yellow tie. We met as a troupe once a week; a young woman was our Captain. When the weather was good, we went camping for a day, and cooked over a campfire and hiked several miles. That was my favorite activity. Twice when I was 10 and 11, my sister and I went to a big Girl Guide camp where real town girls came from 20 or 50 miles away. We slept in assigned groups in a row of tents, in a different section of the lake, ten miles from home.

Our meals were in a long shed with tables and benches. At night we had a big bonfire and sang the old songs. My sister, three years older, was very popular. She sang well and played her ukulele — a very outgoing girl — and I was proud of her, and also a little jealous.

I was shy and introverted, but still had some new friends whose lives were so different from mine. It was a good experience even though once I was invalided. I went home midweek with tonsillitis. Those were pre-antibiotic days. It took ten days before I felt well enough to get up and out. My mother, bless her, used to soak a cloth in vinegar and put it around my neck, as a cure.

Also, she believed in eggnog with raw eggs whipped in milk, which I didn't like and I poured it down the toilet if I could. Ungrateful little wretch I was. In fact, my mother had to treat so many cuts, bites and infections, she was an expert. There was no doctor or vet around. We had a neighbor who had been a medic in World War I, and had been shell shocked and stuttered badly. He would be summoned in the worst cases and gave advice as well as he could. When they — he and my mother — concluded their session, he always offered her a nip of scotch that he carried around! That really gave her a much-needed lift.

Edwin

My brother was always called Ed except by his father. He was the oldest in our family of seven children. He grew up almost in another generation from myself, six years younger. Somehow, because he was a quiet person, he always was respected by us all, even his parents. I can't remember his ever being rebuffed or criticized. An astounding feat by my standards. I was always in a tussle with my brother who was younger than me, or being reprimanded by my parents. If Ed ever spoke to me, I was elated. So he grew up, wasn't given any favors, but never caused any trouble. Maybe even as a kid he was eminently sensible.

When he was about 16 he started to go out with girls. Not our neighbors but someone farther away so we never saw who she was. He was mechanically inclined and could fix anything, and was in demand by my mother to fix a clock or sharpen knives. He could do very neat carpentry also, which he learnt the usual way, by following the hired men from a young age and doing what they did.

The thing I remember best was his bug. This was what he built from the Model T Ford that sat unused in our garage. He made it into a bug by building an open body onto the chassis and painting it red. In all of this he was helped by his best friend, Halsey, an older boy who was destined to fix cars, even those unfixable, during his whole life!

Ed and his red bug were very popular. During the late 30s, cars were few and far between, gas was cheap. I remember Ed driving his dad one day to the train. My dad, a very nervous and high-strung man, had perfect confidence in his son, and looked quite relaxed sitting in the passenger seat.

During the late 30's gold mining started up in the Yukon Territories North of British Columbia. That was where jobs could be found. There was no work close to home. Ed and Halsey made the trip first to Seattle, then by boat to Skagway, and from there to Dawson in the Yukon.

They drove water pipes down through the permafrost to a depth of four feet and then steam was forced through the pipes to thaw the soil. The big machines followed, picking up mud and sending it through slides that washed out the gold. The work was hard but the pay was good.

Work began in June and ended in September. Then everything froze up for the long winter. Ed and Halsey, like all the other men, made the journey back to the boat, flush with their earnings. Many of them gambled all their earnings away on the boat trip. Ed and Halsey were too smart. They were able to buy gifts for their parents and have enough to go back to the gold fields the following year.

In 1939 the Second World War started on September 3. Most of the young men signed up, if only to get free room and board and a few dollars of their own. Ed and Halsey were reluctant to join up. They were doing well in the Yukon. However, two years later, mainly because all their friends were gone, they did join the military. Ed was in the 1st Canadian infantry or, as he called it, "cannon fodder." Halsey was in the ordnance corps because he could fix the tanks.

Ed was shipped to England and on D-Day was one of the vast forces of allied nations to be catapulted into France. He was lucky enough to reach foxholes one by one until he ended up, after three solid months of this kind of war, in Holland. He was taken off active duty and kept in Holland. He got back to England and after a night of drinking ended up in a gutter, unconscious. Whoever found him got him to a hospital. He nearly died of pneumonia then, which was ironic since he had survived the fighting with no wound.

When Ed got back from the war he spoke of it very little. But I noticed that in subsequent years he never again went hunting or fishing. As a teenager he had enjoyed these pursuits. I guess the horror and heartlessness of his experience left him with a greater regard for living things.

He got married to Helen, a girl he had known in Dawson and

they had three boys. He went to the University of British Columbia and got a masters in marine biology. He became Minister of Fisheries in BC. He died at age 72, relatively young, but he had been a heavy smoker.

Muña

Muña was the sister next to me. She was older by two and a half years. I admired her. She was my protector in case of bullies and was often in a knock-down rolling-about fight with big girls she had argued with. She always won because of her strength and agility.

When she was in her teens, she got a guitar and learned to play chords and she sang. She had a good, clear soprano voice. She was always singing, always in tune. I had no voice and could not hold a tune.

When we went to the big summer Girl Scout camp, she was always leading the singing around the campfire. I admit that though I was proud of her I was also jealous of her popularity.

So we grew.

She was a natural rider and horsewoman. She had a pony called Toby, a treacherous little beast he could be. He always tried to buck us off or sideswipe us against the fence. Muña could control him best.

When she left the farm to go to work in Vancouver, I was his chief rider and had quite a few tumbles. It ended up that after I left home nobody rode him and he went wild. One day he got out and became a part, even a leader, of a group of wild horses on the Indian reservation. I hope he enjoyed his freedom and didn't starve to death in the cold winters.

Muña taught riding to young people in a job she had in the city. She took them out in the big Stanley Park on trails through the woods. She later worked in a girls' boarding school, teaching the girls riding.

During this time, she acquired a horse she called "Bing." He was not a beauty, but he could jump. She raced him in gymkhanas, and he always won the obstacle courses, sailing over hedges and jumps and pools without effort.

Muña won many cups with Bing and it was a thrill to watch as they went into the competition. It all stopped in a few years. The American teams came with more expensive horses and took all the prizes. Muña didn't, and could not, compete on such a level, but she had won a lot of prizes.

She moved to a ranch with her new husband, and they raised two children. Every summer the cousins would come to the ranch and Muña would take care of them all. As they became teenagers they helped outside with the haying and other chores. They all enjoyed it.

As she got older, she remained alone on the ranch. She and her husband separated, and he moved away. It was always a friendly place to visit and Muña loved to talk. She smoked too much and got emphysema. She caught a nasty cold and would not go to the doctor. She died of galloping pneumonia. She was 67 years old.

School

The Depression of the 30's was the decade in which I spent most of my time in primary school. In fact, it was the only school in the whole district. It had to be more or less in the centre since all the kids and the teacher walked there. A few rode horses in summer. The teacher taught all of us, from kindergarten to eighth grade. Some boys, I remember, in the eighth grade were 15 or 16 and as tall as men. But the diminutive teacher kept them and all of us in order. There was an unquestioning discipline.

In the school year, there were two occasions that everyone enjoyed: the Christmas concert and the school picnic at the end of the school year in June. The picnic was organized by parents, those who were trustees. It was held at a distance in a place where we could swim, run, and explore fields and woods — a place to build a fire for cooking hotdogs.

All the foods were laid out by mothers, the fathers tended fires and marked the races. We ran, had jumps, sack races, and three-legged races. I always tried mightily to win, unless overcome by laughter in the three-legged when we fell down.

There's a photo my mother took at one picnic of five girls, each holding to her chest a huge bouquet of wildflowers. They had picked and picked in a field of lupins, paintbrush, and chocolate lilies. One cannot find these anymore in such quantities — human growth has obliterated them.

All these activities were followed by hotdogs and lunch of salads of many kinds. The big boys ate six or seven hotdogs with no trouble. I can't remember any obese kids, and on that day, we ate prodigiously. The dessert of chocolate cake and homemade ice-cream was the crowning luxury of the day.

After everyone rinsed their own plate and spoon in the lake, preparations were made to break up, clean up all debris, and pack for home. As we had come, most went in wagons. In the whole district there were only two cars. It had been a fine day.

My Best Teacher

I went to elementary school during the 1930s. It was a one-room school including grades one to eight. Altogether about 15 children from mostly farm families, kids who walked maybe from half a mile to three miles to get there.

During the entire time, including grades one to eight, I had one teacher, Miss Grant. She boarded with a family about a mile and a half away. She was a little person with pretty red hair, basically shy, but that aspect was not visible to us children. We knew her as a good friend, but also a good disciplinarian. We couldn't get away with much. We'd be talking or passing notes, and suddenly you'd feel a "wham" on the side of the face where she had walked up behind and caught us in the act.

Punishment meant staying after school and writing lines like "I must not talk or write notes" up to 100 times. Then she'd check that it was right before telling the culprit to go home. Everyone was fairly treated. She didn't favor any of us. There were some big boys in the eighth grade and the diminutive Miss Grant was able to discipline them too, and they responded to her. We learned a lot, by today's standards. I still remember the names and capitals of most countries, their important products and their biggest rivers. In Canada we learned all the kings of Britain, and the less eventful Canadian history. We learned composition and could parse any sentence word by word. I can't remember what books we read because I read everything I could get my hands on. Miss Grant was responsible for it all. Year after year she spent with us, our only teacher.

Every Valentine's Day we had a shoe box all decorated with a slit in the top. We made Valentines and put the recipient's name on, but not our own. Someone would open the box and they would be given out. It was good fun, sometimes even the teacher got some. She would pass out candies, so it was a little festive and way more fun than schoolwork.

I didn't realize it until I became an adult, but Miss Grant was a good teacher and everyone liked her, even if she had punished us for being cheeky or disobedient. She left to get married the year after I finished eighth grade. She married a very shy but good man, and I heard that they had five or six children.

The Neighbors at Sorrento

In those days, the neighborhood did not change much, and people all stayed and persevered in the day-to-day work of life. Except for an old person dying, or a baby being born (and not many of those) we all just went on.

Our nearest neighbors had a little log house that they had built themselves. He grew a big nursery garden and sold plants. He grew a lot of lavender. You could smell it all around their place. There was a market for it in the East. His wife made bread, lots of it. Often my mother sent us running through the woods to her house for a loaf of bread. Someone had come to visit us and we didn't have quite enough for the dinner. We were a big family as it was, and got through prodigious amounts of food. Mrs. K was always gracious about it. She said she always made a spare loaf for our family. Usually there was only herself and her husband.

We had one very special neighbor. His family had come to the area years before ours. But one of his daughters grew up with my two older sisters. Walter was often summoned to our house to fix things. He was a godsend for that reason. My father was not practical, and depended on Walter to keep things going. He fixed machinery, did plumbing, amused us kids with magic and card tricks and Paul Bunyon stories. He also brought us a bag of candies every time. At Christmas he would hitch up his team to a wagon-sleigh, put lots of straw in the wagon bed, and take all the area kids for a sleigh ride. We would come home in the dark and get dropped off in front of our places. It was a lovely experience.

There was Bert Anderson. He had lost his wife, and brought his little girl of six to live with us for a year while he got over some of his grief. She was the same age as my younger brother. She fit in just fine with us all and went back home when her father had found a stepmother for her. We saw her every day at school and on holidays she played often at our place. Mr. A also had an orchard and managed several others. He hired us in the fall to pick apples. We had to be at least 14, and we would pick all day while the job lasted. We made good money, two dollars an hour. So at the end we got a nice sum. One year I spent it on a new coat from Eaton's catalog. The second year, I went to Vancouver to visit my elder sister: I spent it on warm clothes and shoes, and the train fare there and back. It was my first time in a real city and it was very exciting.

A bit farther away lived my favorite family. The two girls were good friends to my sister and me. Their mother, Mrs. P, was the life of every party. She was full of life and energy, and was always laughing heartily. She arranged plays, wrote them herself, and we performed them for the neighborhood to enjoy. It was fun, and a lot of adults helped us with costumes. We practiced a lot because Mrs P was expecting us to do our parts well. The plays were a big success, thanks to her. She also had a car with a rumble seat, and took us for rides, which we loved, all crowded into that rumble seat like sardines.

Among other neighbors, Miss Coates was also more needy than the others. I often was sent to help her weed her vegetable garden and do chores. She in return would give me a dime. That seemed enough pay for a ten-year-old and I would deposit it in my piggy bank. My family called me the miser because I saved my various small salaries.

Miss Coates had a horse called Daisy and she would hitch her to a light wagon called a "democrat" and go to buy her supplies and also to visit in the neighborhood. In the winter Daisy pulled her in a small sleigh. She was known chiefly for her herd of some 25 cats. Every night she would call them each by name, and cats would scamper after her from everywhere like she was the Pied Piper.

She sometimes asked me into her house. My main memory of it was the gloom. It never seemed light inside. She would give me tea and shortbread made with rancid butter. I usually managed to conceal the shortbread in a corner or in a pocket. Once she gave me a book called Hereward the Wake, The Last of the English.

The print was small and I had difficulty reading it. I still have that book. I am sure it would be interesting for someone interested in old English history.

Looking back, I think that Miss Coates was, in her weird way, a brave little soul, even though people laughed at her behind her back. Sometimes it was hard not to.

The Characters of My Childhood

Perhaps because of the relative isolation, or because those were the times before psychology and sociology, it seems as though we had an overabundance of odd people. Some, one could be sorry for, others were just plain funny. People visited us quite freely, out of friendliness or loneliness. One lady would walk two miles from her farm. She said her husband and son never talked to her and she would get so lonely. My mother would be working in her flower garden and Mrs. Dilly would talk and talk about nothing in particular. To suggest that it was time to go (after two boring hours) my mother would pick a bouquet of flowers for her. Mrs. Dilly just went on talking and pulling all the petals off her bouquet absentmindedly while my mother stared at her in horror. Finally, she would wander off. Then my mother usually said to us, "The poor soul."

We only had one man with dark skin in the area and he was called "N——— Taylor." Our family liked him; we called him George. He would come over and talk for an hour or so through the open window. He laughed a lot. He lived by the lake in a tiny cabin. As children we would visit him and have a good talk about animals. He once trapped a bobcat that had been eating our lambs. We were very grateful. In the winter he went somewhere else, hopefully to a warmer place. He was chatty and a decent man.

In a pretty isolated part lived two men, both bachelors, in their respective houses. They were friends and once in a while would walk to our store to get their provisions. One of them put an ad in the personal column of the paper, asking for a housekeeper — "object matrimony." He got one all right but she married his friend instead. I never knew how he felt about that. Perhaps he got the better part of the deal!

There was Mr. Levy who lived quite near us, his fence right next to ours in one corner. He would lean over his gate and talk to people passing by on the main road. Every night when we brought in the cows and sheep he would be there. My little brother liked to talk too so they had long chats. He grew bees and would give my brother the honeycombs. He showed him how he extracted the honey. My brother brought home honey and the waxy honeycomb. We chewed it like chewing gum. Mr. Levy never let anyone in his house, they said. Someone once told us that many years before in another place, he had killed a man with a rock. It may explain his wish to keep to himself.

Flowers from My Childhood

Spring brings back memories of wildflowers that were so plentiful in open places, in untilled fields, and in the woods around our farm and those of our neighbors. Some of these places we kept secret. We didn't want too many people tramping around or picking the flowers. It was a way to preserve the shyest of the wildflowers, like the delicate pink lady slippers. They were hidden in deep woods in mossy damp places under big trees, for the shade was necessary. Such a lovely treat to come on a small group of lady slippers in such a hidden spot.

If it were around Mothers's Day, we would pick a few flowers on their four-inch stems to bring home. Our mother loved them, but was always too busy to spend time wandering in the woods in search of these secretive flowers.

Another orchid plant we might find was called the yellow moccasin. I think in my entire childhood we only found three or four of these clumps. They were bigger, the moccasin part being yellow, two inches long, and an inch wide. They were lovely too, but more sturdy looking, and almost awesome in their rarity. Once my older siblings dug up an entire clump and transplanted them in our garden. The following year nothing came up, not one shoot or leaf.

Other flowers were more easily found. We could bring home lots of what we called johnny jump-ups but in the flower book were called trout lilies. They were small lilies, yellow with white tips. There was an old field full of them. We made a trip to that field once every spring to pick a bouquet or two of these pretty flowers. It was a two- or three-mile walk each way, so we didn't undertake the trip lightly.

Those were the early spring flowers we treasured. The summer ones were the blue lupins and Indian paintbrush, still plentiful today in unploughed corners of ranches.

In older times, chocolate lilies were found among them, but I haven't seen any of these for many years. The flowers are a bright brown and look like little bells on a long stalk. Each flower is round, about ½ an inch in diameter, and quite lovely. I haven't seen them mentioned in flower books. It would be strange if they grew only in the early clearings of British Columbia.

There may have been other beautiful flowers but the ones I have mentioned are the ones I remember best. Sunflowers and asters are ubiquitous but still a fine sight on a hillside or roadside.

Teen Age

As a teenager, my life got more complicated, as everyone's does, I think. I didn't have, after finishing eighth grade, a school to go to. There was as yet no high school in the area, and it seemed lonely, in spite of my big family and many chores. I started to take home-study courses in ninth grade at home. They were sent every two weeks from government headquarters in Victoria. The student was responsible for the books needed for each course, and for the assignments in each paper, and for sending in the completed papers. In turn, someone corrected them, made recommendations and remarks, and gave a letter A, B, C, or whatever grade I received. I took all the required courses by mail, for each grade, following the school year, right up to 12th when I graduated.

The graduation exams were held in a high school in the nearest town 20 miles away. I stayed overnight in the town hotel and after doing the exams along with the town students, I came home on the greyhound bus. I don't remember talking to anyone at school or in town. I had no friends there. The best part I remember was sitting at the counter in the local restaurant blissfully tucking away a giant banana split!

Looking back on the high school, which I completed, I don't remember discussing any of it with my family, or with friends. It was my solitary effort and interest that got me through. From today's standpoint it would be unheard of! We are so verbal about everything now. I can only say in retrospect, it worked for me, a rather odd teenager.

My sisters and I often went up the nearby mountains on a Sunday. We would carry a lunch and go right to the top. Some of the tops were rocky and open and we could see our farm spread out far below. Other tops were densely wooded, or flat, and you couldn't look out. There were mountain sheep up there; we would see them running around the cliffs and rocks. It was always a thrill to see them as they jumped from rock to crag. We had a special mountain that we would climb with our friends. We called it "Misty Ridge." We would make a campfire and cook hotdogs or biscuits there. Even after we grew up and left home, when we came back to visit, we would try and make a hike up to Misty Ridge.

World War II came to Canada in 1939. I was 15. Everyone was asked to register, and I remember asking to be an ambulance driver. I could drive a tractor and figured that was enough. Anyhow, no one ever called me up. The young men were joining up because employment in the Depression was so scarce. They were greatly missed. We had a local badminton club and our best players were gone. One of my friends and I used to play each other on weekend mornings, just for fun and sociability. The girls in our family had to do the fieldwork because we couldn't get hired help anymore.

I had a friend who lived across the lake and seven miles past. I would visit her on my bike. She was a very individual girl, with her own opinions, which she talked about freely. Her political views were quite radical too, and I marveled at her independence of thought and how she expressed it. Once, in late summer we went together up into the high alpine meadows of the mountains behind her farm. We were on horses, and we led a packhorse with our bedrolls, food and cooking utensils for a campfire. It was a stiff climb up a well-worn trail, but after a few hours we came out on an alpine meadow, dense with flowers of all sorts. The snow stays up there until June, so the growing season is brief, over in September, as it gets cold and snow falls again. It was lovely up there. We kept our eyes peeled for grizzlies, which came up there too for berries and small animals. We stayed two or three nights, until our food gave out, and we couldn't find any good things to eat, like roots or berries.

On the way down I did see a grizzly. A young one passed across the trail in front of me, and disappeared into the woods. The horses snorted and shied, but soon forgot it. At least I'd seen a bear. No one was home at Lib's house so we unpacked, and being very hungry, picked a lot of green beans in her garden. We cooked and ate them and felt nicely satisfied. Later that day I left my friend and went back home. It had been a fine adventure.

So passed my teens at Sorrento. I was backward socially compared to my sisters. They were invited to dances by boys, and were popular and pretty. I never was, and it bothered me, of course, and made me more interested in study and books to compensate. Trouble was, I didn't really know how to talk to or even flirt with the young men, and they didn't interest me enough. I think a lot of it was delayed hormones. In my very late teens I began to bloom more, and that's when I noticed men looking at me. But that was after I had left home for Vancouver, which is another story entirely.

Making Hay

In those relatively short summers we got in Sorrento, roughly from June to early September, the biggest job was haymaking. There were fields of mostly alfalfa plus timothy grass and whatever else grew there to be cut, raked into windrows, then into haycocks, all the time drying in the sun.

Rain wouldn't help so sometimes it was a race to get the hay into the barn while it was still dry. During our teens, which was wartime, this job was ours. Everyone else had joined up and were being sent to Europe.

We worked with horses so we knew how to do all the parts of the hay making. When it came to bringing in the crop we loaded up the hayrack. One person was on top dispersing the pitchforks-full handed up to make a wide flat load. Two people pitched up, and the person on top would drive the horses ahead. When the load was high enough, everyone would climb onto the load and we would drive to the side of the barn open to the loft.

One of us remained on the load and one would go in the loft. The third would unhook the horses, drive them to the back of the barn and hook them to a pulley, which extended to a track at the top of the barn and through to the other side, then down to a wide fork. This fork was pushed into the load at an angle and clamped shut so it held onto its load.

Then the person on the load who had manipulated the fork hollered 'OK!" or "Right!" The horses were driven ahead and pulled, via the pulley, the load around the fork up to the track at the top of the barn. There it connected with a loud click, and was drawn into the barn when the person in the loft called out 'Right!" loudly. The horses stopped. The person on the load pulled on a rope attached to the fork. It opened the tines of the fork so that its load dropped into the loft.

The one in the loft moved the load to where it was flat so the loft was filled evenly and the hay was tramped down. Then the one on the hayload pulled on his rope and brought the fork down. This whole process was repeated until the hay rack was bare. Maybe that took about eight or nine fork loads if the load was built up well while in the field.

It was tiring and quite hot sometimes. We would go out to the field and in the middle of the afternoon we'd sit in the shade and rest. My mother or a little sister would bring us lemonade. Delicious rest! Then we would continue till after five and call it a day. There was still the milking at six. We had supper at seven. Often we would then go to the lake, a mile away, but so refreshing in the evening.

So it would go, one hayload after another, one field after another. The weather was mostly good, and we could dodge the rain which came mostly at night, hopefully when no hay was drying in the field. Moldy hay in the winter was not healthy for the cows. It was really bad for horses, for their lungs. It made their breathing loud and no doubt difficult. They worked hard and deserved good feed. The milk cows needed good hay. The poorer hay was given to the dry stock which were yearlings, steers, young heifers.

By September, somehow the barns were full, winter feed was assured, and we put away the mower, the big rakes, and our pitchforks and loafed for a week. Soon there were other jobs to turn to.

Mountaineering on the Elephant's Toes

We set off after all our chores were done, and after a good breakfast. We had two big sandwiches wrapped in waxed paper, a thermos full of cold water, and several man-sized handkerchiefs filched from our Dad. These would make good bandages in case of cuts or scrapes, or, if tied together, a decent sling for sprains. Not that we expected to use them, but better safe than sorry.

The walk to the foot of the mountain was about two miles. We were going to climb a big bluff called the Elephant's Toes because there were three rocky bumps with no trees on them and above the bumps the rise was greener and not so steep, as seen from the ground.

There was a pretty good trail leading up to a low ridge where there was a flat place with a big pine tree. From there you could look down on the farms, roads, and the slope that rolled gently to the lake. It all looked like a toy spread before us. Facing the mountain we could see the Elephant's Toes and a few dead trees, still black from last year's fire.

As we toiled up the steep side of these humps on a narrow trail we looked over the rocks to see a wonderful sight. There was a big ram with curling horns on either side of his head jumping nimbly from crag to crag. Five or six sheep followed him. All gleamed white in the sun. They had scented us and were running off. This was their territory and they knew every nook and crag. It was a lovely sight but soon they all disappeared, far off to safety.

We climbed slowly up and got past the open crags into low shrubs and long grass. We called it deer grass as it was native, and had never been disturbed from its own habitat. I guess it made a good meal for the mountain sheep. There was a summit, or so we thought, but it turned out not to be because as we came over it, another rose before us. At last, we stood on the top.

It was flat for about 100 yards on each side, and before us. There were sheep trails through the low shrubbery, and a few bigger trees. We were, as we knew, not at the altitude above 4000 feet where trees got stunted. But it was plenty high for us, and we looked about for a nice spot to rest and eat our sandwiches.

As we roamed about, we came across a sunken area and there we saw a fine sight. A little lake, pristine and blue, surrounded by low willows, lay before us. It was about 50 feet across and almost round, with an open spot where we could sit. What a lovely surprise. We felt like Lewis and Clark, the first white people to cross the Rockies.

Migration

We were on our late summer camping trip. After traveling up the highway into Northern British Columbia for three days, we had come to a series of big lakes in the lee of the towering Rockies. We camped in a grove of pines, clearing away layers of sweet-scented needles to pitch the tent. It was not a prepared campsite.

We made a fire and cooked stew and coffee, rinsing out our blackened pots in the nearby lake. The water was clear and cold. The night was starry. Perfect.

We noticed earlier that small flocks of wild geese kept coming in and landing on the lake. Loud squawks ensued. Perhaps they were introducing themselves to the crowd already assembled. Finally, all was silent on the lake as the assembled birds rested, packed in among each other for protection.

The next morning we were awakened before the sunrise. The geese were restlessly swimming about, squawking raucously in a cacophony of sound. As we watched, suddenly as if on signal, they all rose and flew around the lake a few times and then settled back into the water with a noisy splash.

After about ten minutes the whole exercise was repeated with a huge racket. On the third try, they finally must have felt that all was right, for off they went, forming a giant 'V' in the sky, honking all the time.

At last they disappeared away South. They would have a long voyage to the Southern US where they would regain their fat over the winter.

As we thought of these intrepid creatures, it seemed we had been privy to watching ancient rites, and it made us feel humble and hushed as we too got up and broke camp.

Going to Vancouver

In the summer of 1942, when I was 18, I had a talk with my father about what to do with my life. He was about to go to Ottawa where he had a job translating letters of German war prisoners to their families. These had to be censored by the government. I was at a loss and said I was interested in biology. He suggested getting books from the University of British Columbia library, and writing to some places like agricultural experiment stations and fisheries in British Columbia. So I did that. To my surprise, I was offered a job at the Pacific Fisheries Experiment Station in Vancouver. The job was for someone who would wash the laboratory glassware and take care of a rat colony. I was overjoyed!

I moved to Vancouver in November. My older sister, Bets, said the first thing was to get a room to live in. For a week I trailed after her in search of a room, trying the layout of the streets. Everything was new and strange to me. After a week my sister got fed up and said she'd had enough. I could jolly well get on with finding my own room. She had other things to do! So I did. In two days I found a little attic room with a bed, a hot plate, table and chair and a bureau. Fine I thought, and settled in. From there I could walk to work.

In those first months I felt very happy and optimistic and did my best keeping glassware sparkling and the rats flourishing. Then I was able to do a few things in the lab of one of the research men. He quickly trained me to be a technician and for three years I did just that, and enjoyed it. During this time I went to night school, and got my senior matriculation, which corresponds to first year of university.

For my recreation I would go skiing. My sister and her husband took me at first, as they were avid skiers. Then I became friends with sisters who had their own cabin. I joined them and we would go up on Saturdays, ski all day Sunday and come home dead tired. It was good fun while I was working but I couldn't manage the expenses when at U.B.C, as I needed to work on Saturdays. Then my boss suggested that I go to university and apply for a bursary for my expenses.

So I went, and I majored in bacteriology and biochemistry in the Faculty of Agriculture.

I worked part-time for my living expenses and books. I worked in the university library on weekends and at odd times during the week, and I did waitressing. In my last year I worked as a lab assistant in biology classes.

Those were happy times because I had the company of the students for the first time since grade school. They were a mix of girls who had gone to university straight from high school, and older ones who had joined the Women's Army and now the war was over, they could continue their education.

I met my brother Ed there. I was in my senior year and he was a freshman. After several years in the army he could continue his education along with many other veterans. When I graduated I was 24.

A number of us went on a week's ski trip to what is now a hotel complex ski area, but which then was totally undeveloped. We lived in tents and packed in our packs over our clothes. Food and sleeping bags were flown in and dropped in the camp. It was May so days were not cold. There was lots of snow. We all had a good time. I remember being glad to get home and have a good shower! That was our graduation!

Picking Fruit

It is late summer now and my mind goes back to my youth and picking apples.

Our farm was next to a big apple orchard. From age 14 and up we were hired on for about three weeks to pick. Hours were eight to five with an hour off for lunch. We felt great to be making a real wage, I believe 50 cents an hour at that time. I knew exactly how I would spend whatever I accrued at the finish.

We wore a picking bag over our shoulders, hanging in front. When it was full we climbed off the ladder and emptied it by unhooking a clasp and opening the bottom into a wooden apple box. Then we rehooked the clasp back up for the next load which would fill the next box, and so on.

The mornings were fresh and chilly, and the later hours warm, sunny and beautiful. Each picker took a tree and picked it all. Sometimes my brother would come with his friends and they would compete with each other. They would bump the apples into the boxes and goodness knows what they didn't do. If the owner was around he would reprimand them severely, which helped for a while. In general, we worked hard and we were glad to be rehired each fall.

In a later year, after the university closed in May, I went to the Okanagan Valley to pick fruit for a summer. That was a region about 100 miles south of Sorrento where cherries, peaches and apricots could be grown in orchards, and didn't get frost-killed in winter. The orchards surrounded Okanagan Lake, which was famous for its legendary serpent called the Ogopogo. People claim to have seen it, a big black serpentine form undulating across the lake. I never saw a sign of it.

I started with cherry picking. For the first two days I ate vast quantities but after that I couldn't bear even one. The owners never chastised us for eating them because they knew it wouldn't last long.

When the cherries were over I went to a peach orchard and there you couldn't pick the green ones. You had to pick softly, rolling the fruit into your palm, trying not to leave any fingerprints on the skin. I caught on and became an expert in a few days. After peaches came apricots, they had to be picked carefully too.

By the end of August I was finished, and went home for a few days before going back to another year of university. I certainly had a healthy summer in the fresh air, eating good country food and sleeping soundly at night.

In Montreal

When I was finishing my third year of University, I discussed with my professors the chances of getting a summer job. He enthusiastically suggested a firm in Montreal that took laboratory help, even from British Columbia. I got a summer job there, and soon found myself on a train going across Canada. It was my first time out of BC, so it was quite exciting. It took four days.

I had an upper berth for the night and I remember sleeping quite soundly. One morning when I woke I looked out the window and saw a moose eating in a sort of swamp, trees all around. I knew then we had crossed the prairies and I was in North Ontario, only one day from Montreal.

On arrival I stayed at the YWCA, a nice building, well used. It was a safe starting place for I knew no one. I walked to the top of Mount Royal, not a very great height but enough to see the city spread out on all sides with the St. Lawrence River sparkling through on its way to Three Rivers and towns on the edges of Ontario.

Everyone rode the streetcars. There were very few cars in the days after World War II. The conductors were French and that's what they spoke as they announced the stops. Every streetcar had a sign saying, "Defense de Cracher," meaning "no spitting." I found my workplace, a large complex in the area called St. Laurent. Everyone said "San Lauron," i.e. the French pronunciation.

Right away, as you walked toward the labs, you could smell horse very strongly. One product they manufactured was Premarin." Women used it to reduce menopausal symptoms. I don't know if it is still used. It was made from pregnant mares' urine and that's why there was always the horse smell.

I enjoyed the lab work. We were working in small groups, testing new antibiotics. They were producing streptomycin and we tested the different batches. There were standard tests and we followed the procedures very precisely. The leader of our group was very intelligent and pleasant and kept us all getting along together. She became a dear friend right through the rest of my life.

I lived only about a half-hour from work. I had moved into a small bungalow owned by two sisters. They were French-Canadian but spoke English well and treated me as a friend. They sometimes took me to their parents' home in the Laurentian Mountains. These were low mountains on the North side of Montreal across the river. The parents lived about 40 miles away. The family was interesting. Their father had been a sea captain in France. Their mother was Austrian, had come to France and met their father, and together they came to Canada. They had a small farm and raised three sons and three daughters. The girls were working as secretaries in the city where I met them. They had advertised for a paying housemate.

I enjoyed living with those girls; we were around the same age. They discussed boyfriends and I did too so we had things in common. I would ski with them in the mountains when they visited their parents. Because I felt well there I prolonged my stay and worked a whole year while I enjoyed everything — even the intensely cold Eastern winter. Everyone wore either furs or warm wool and warm hats. Otherwise, we would freeze.

The following summer I returned to BC in order to finish my final year to get a BSA (Bachelor of Science in Agriculture). The time in Montreal had opened my eyes to many new possibilities, as long as I could get good jobs.

My Good Friend

When I was in my early twenties I went from British Columbia to live in Montreal. I had a job there working as a lab assistant in a company making antibiotics. My immediate boss was Ethel.

She headed a small group of us doing tests of various antibiotics. She was a cheery, very intelligent and warm-hearted young woman, two or three years my senior. Everyone liked her.

She was a good organizer, a good worker and we all worked as a team with no ill feeling at all, which was almost miraculous. I had worked in groups that had tension due to unspoken unfriendly feelings among staff. Ethel had, however, a way with her.

During my 15-month stay in Montreal, Ethel got married. On the bus bringing her to work she had met her future husband. It was when the bus broke down one day, and they were all standing around, that he got up the courage to speak to her. Three months later they were married. And it was a lovely marriage. Ethel said she had many difficulties in her long life, but her marriage was always like a rock.

She and Irving became my good friends for life. The thing

that was so endearing was her capacity to listen to my troubles, and at the end to make a gentle tactful comment that would point the way to a solution I needed to make. She would listen to other friends too who, like myself, trusted her implicitly.

Over the course of our lives we were separated by geography but kept in touch now and then. If I was traveling near where she lived, I would drop in and stay for a day or two. She and Irving, I decided, were old souls.

Irving died when he was 80. Ethel called me on the phone, and I found myself crying, which I don't often do. Two years ago her daughter Deborah called me to say her mother had died on Christmas Day. She was 89. She was a great lady.

After University Ends

When I graduated from UBC I needed a job for the simple reason that I needed to buy food and shelter. I answered an ad for a graduate in microbiology at the University of Saskatchewan. They accepted my application and I found myself, suitcase in hand, hitchhiking over the Rockies.

These were the days when hitchhiking was safe. I got rides till near Saskatchewan, and then I took a bus the last few miles. I travelled about four days in all. I arrived in Saskatoon safely and found a room to rent in a private house. It was not far from the university where I would be working. The town was not big, about 50,000 people. You could walk all through it in an hour or less. It was very flat. Of course, everywhere you looked the whole countryside was flat. After living my entire life in mountainous British Columbia, I felt exposed, unsheltered even.

But then there were compensations. In my job, which was in the bacteriology, mold and fungus study, I enjoyed my friendly boss and even an eager assistant. We were screening molds from my boss's collection from a trip he made to the Amazon River and bordering countries. We were searching for antibiotics inspired by Fleming's discovery of penicillin from a mold he found growing on a grapefruit in his refrigerator. It felt like we were looking for gold and it spurred us on.

It got very cold in the winter there. It would go down to 40 degrees below Fahrenheit and stay there for three or four weeks. It would be sunny and still, no blizzards or wind. I got used to it but when I walked 15 minutes to work, the tip of my nose would turn white — probably frozen!

There was an indoor skating rink at the university and I would skate energetically before or after work. In the summer I played tennis, and my game improved a lot. I also joined a women's softball team at the local YWCA. When I was young that organization was flourishing as a place where newcomers might stay, and join groups, go swimming and find companionship.

Saskatoon had gardens, shrubs and lots of bushes along the river which ran through the middle of it. I had a very pleasant life there. It was only the flatness and lack of trees that I missed.

Once I went North on a bus trip, about 200 miles to the treeline, in search of trees. I found them, hundreds in an impenetrable forest, growing tightly together, a solid wall but not tall. About 7-8 feet high, perhaps a little more, a stunted forest. It was colder up there, and trees would not grow any taller. That was a disappointment.

In the fall, for my vacation, I took a bus trip to the East, through Manitoba, Ontario, and the Maritimes. I saw trees again, great maples, sycamores, and oaks. I seemed to drink in the sight like a wanderer in a desert who comes upon an oasis. It was wonderful to see all those tall trees again. It is amazing, yet natural, to miss such things so much if one is deprived of them.

Settling Down

My husband, my two-year-old daughter, and I moved into a house in Armonk, NY in 1960. We had started to fix up the old farmhouse, about 100-plus years old. A very simple house, three small bedrooms and a bathroom upstairs and a living room, dining room and a small kitchen downstairs. We also had two acres of woods behind,

It was still a little rough outside, but gradually we were able to remove old glass, cans and rubbish, and made it nice enough so we could have picnics outside. Neighbors came to pay respects, the old timers and a few families who were involved with IBM. Its headquarters were in Armonk.

Gradually newer people moved in around us. People out of New York, Brooklyn and the Bronx, heavily populated areas. People of Italian and mid-European backgrounds. They were happy to move to the far suburbs for a little privacy.

When we first came we joined a little rag-taggle group of Democrats. We went to a picnic and played a sort of baseball. They told us that the old timers in Armonk were all staunch Republicans.

The democrats were mostly Irish and Jewish employees newly arrived, working for IBM.

My husband and I liked the old timers because of the ease and assurance of being right. Even though we didn't share political beliefs, we enjoyed their company. People told us that when New York natives moved up to Armonk that they changed from being Democrats to being Republicans. It made them feel more secure because then they were well connected with the old timers.

We Dems, as we called ourselves, always ran candidates for Town Supervisor, and for Councilmen. We always lost. But it was fun anyway. We gave coffee hours to introduce our candidates. We made posters and put them down in the village. No dice. The place was firmly Republican. But strangely enough, 30 years later when we had left the area, old friends told us that Armonk had finally gone to the Democrats.

1200 Park Avenue and I

I came to live here in April of 2010. I had been living for most of my life in New York and Connecticut. But having been born and raised in BC, Canada, I could still feel an affinity with the West and its free manner of living. And Chico was a beautiful small town. I loved the trees -— so many! And so welcome to walk under them on a hot day, and feel the relief of their cool shade. I had good vibes about my surroundings, and I settled happily in my apartment.

At that time, Jill and Eric took care of our building. In fact they treated it with all the love and devotion one would for a baby. Most of the tenants were happy and told me they had moved in at the beginning. In fact, there were still finishing touches to the building to be made. I was at the right end of the country to be near my two younger daughters. That was a very good thing. It was unfortunate that my oldest was left behind in New York, but I knew also that she loved where she lived and the city was close to her heart.

At first, I missed things. I couldn't find good bread. Gradually I got used to the bread made at the Tin Roof. From 1200 Park I could walk to most places downtown, and also, the buses were there to take me most anywhere. I could walk to my favorite Thrift Stores, ARC and Elite Repeat — very necessary if my wardrobe needed replenishing and funds sorely depleted. If I bought a lot of groceries at Safeway or Raleys I could get a taxi very reasonably. A couple of my neighbors at 1200 Park here are friendly, generous, and helpful.

My friends back East still keep in touch, bless them. My oldest daughter in New York manages to spend a few days with me once or twice a year. I miss the ethnic varieties of the New York region, but I must say the California restaurants are almost always tops. Except for pizza. They can't equal the New York pizza, but maybe there aren't enough Italians here.

So with a good base at 1200 Park, I am able to enjoy life and what it offers in Chico and surroundings. I am happy enough to spend my old age here.

About Aging

We all age differently. I think I have been lucky, blessed by good health and good genes. We do have some control over our health. We can do all the good things: eat plenty of fresh vegetables and fruits, and go easy on meat and dairy. It seems that eggs are reinstated in the list of healthy foods. I am glad about that.

The second good habit of aging is exercise. Organized movements like yoga keep our bodies flexible and help with back problems. At the end of the yoga session, deep relaxation is the reward of all the movement. Blissful.

My sister Pr, a year younger than me, likes to swim which also helps her arthritis. The idea of swimming has no appeal for me any more, especially in winter, even if it's indoors in a heated pool. Now I walk every day at least half an hour, usually to go to my garden or to buy supplies.

A walk outside will lift a bad mood and make my spirits lighter if I am low. Cheers me right up! Many older ones here have little dogs. They need to be taken out three times a day, so their owner gets enough exercise just to keep their pets happy.

There are things that take the joy of aging for some of us: Parkinson's, Alzheimer's Disease, Dementia and Cancer. We can't prevent them but gradually we may be able to diminish their effect on us. Others may get a stroke and be confined to a wheelchair. So far I have been lucky to avoid these illnesses. In view of all these negative aspects of aging, it is no wonder people would like to avoid getting older at all.

We can do our best though, in any circumstance:

- Work on mental attitude and keep positive.
- Enjoy ourselves day by day.
- Don't plan too far ahead as we can't control the future.
- Keep interest alive in order to have a full life.
- Don't isolate and take advantage of get-togethers.

Many of us kept working well past 70. We needed the money, and added social security. If you need to keep working, do so with enjoyment. If you are retired, volunteering keeps you involved. I worked till well past 80, enjoying it. I didn't earn much above the minimum. I can manage on my own mostly, but I am lucky to have occasional financial help from my daughters.

So far, my life is good and I am grateful for my good luck.

Waiting for the Bus

One morning I was waiting for the bus, right here at 1200 Park, just across from the Jesus Center. A number of unfortunates — homeless men who go there for free meals — collect at this bus stop even though they mostly aren't going anywhere. It affords them a bit of shelter while they wait for the next meal. An unkempt mostly bearded harmless lot.

One man, greatly in need of a shave, was walking nervously back and forth, vainly searching his pockets for bus fare. No luck. Finally, he stopped in front of me. I probably looked like the most prosperous one there. He asked for a dollar which he said was a co-pay for dentistry he was going to. I gave him a dollar and he looked a little more cheerful, but he still needed the fare. He worked his way through the others and finally went across the street and got his fare from someone. Such a precarious way to live.

Then another old man tried talking to me. He was familiar to me because he always said the same things. I told him I wasn't talking, so he went to the next one, trying with the same opening words. I had seen him many times before, it was always the same.

Then he would ride the bus, probably as far as he could and back. Another pathetic character, the flotsam of society. Then the bus arrived and we all three or four got on for our various destinations.

As I sat there and pondered the goods and evils of our present society, I kept thinking that a social worker could get plenty of material to work with just by waiting for a bus. Especially at the Jesus Center. Or across the street at the bus stop of 1200 Park.

Things We Can Do to Cheer Up Our World

1. Learn to be content with what we can't change about our personal situation by a) being as healthy as we can b) cultivating our best friends c) perhaps thinking of those who have it worse.
2. Finding our interests and developing them. Have hobbies.
3. Be kind to others!
4. Try to listen to opposing points of view.
5. There is a lot we can be humble about in ourselves.
6. Don't listen to sad news stories at night. You will have bad dreams
7. Sometimes all we can do is pray. Pray hard and quietly. It does good and quiets one's feeling of uselessness.
8. HOPE!
9. Preserve your strength to fight another day. Stay out of the rain, the heat and the bitter cold. Guard your strength.
10. Enjoy all you can!

We never know for sure, it may be our very last day! The thought of leaving our world is not cheery, so let's make it a good world.

An Afternoon Walk

It was a Sunday afternoon and I was sitting in my apartment feeling bored and a little lonely. I needed some fresh air. I gathered my keys, a jacket, and set out. The day was sunny and breezy. The neighborhood here is mostly houses and gardens. Pretty safe. First one I meet is a woman I know, walking her tiny dog, a Yorkie. We have a short chat and move on.

Then a neatly dressed white-haired man, straight but a little tottery, passes me and says, "Good afternoon." I say, "Good afternoon to you." He passes on. I turn and watch. He seems a little insecure but carefully he uses the cane to steady himself and tottles off.

In a block or two I stop to greet a man in the corner of his garden. I can see he's planted grass seed and he remarks that it needs rain. "We all need rain," I tell him.

A block or so later I come to a man cleaning his yard. "Do I want some grapefruit?" he asked. "Sure!" I said and waited while he picked two nice heavy ones from his big tree. He put them in a bag and I thanked him. He is a very generous man, and once he had given me tomatoes that he grew.

There is a little park about five blocks away and I cut through it. It has some picnic tables and swings, and a slide and a basketball court. A little girl is swinging, and her mother is just watching. It is very quiet there, because it is Sunday.

I walk as far as a big community garden, fenced in. No one is there. The surrounding area has many growing vegetables, onions, cabbages and greens like spinach. Some beautiful iris. It is part of a big garden project of the "Jesus Center." Later they grow the summer vegetables, like squash and tomatoes. It is quite a project. They sell the produce at the local farmers market.

On the way home I pass a big lemon tree. I find two nice ones on the ground, not bruised or cracked. I put them in my bag. By the time I reach home I am rich. Grapefruit, lemon, and several leaves of spinach. But best of all, I was restored.

Is There Hope for Us?

I need to be aware of my footprint on the earth. I don't wish to tread heavily to squash living things underfoot, to be heedless of the consequences. Being distressed about global warming, both the desecration of our forests and the assault on oceans leaves me exhausted and feeling useless, a tiny dot of humanity in the great sea around me. It's more than a body can bear.

What to do? Well, as I already said, what about my own footprint? I need to start from there. No use cursing the government, they seem to be in a permanent argument. Like arranging the deck chairs on the Titanic! It is almost understandable that in the face of such lack of purpose, that one individual can give up in distress. But maybe at a state level, a county level, a district level, or even less, at an individual level, we can mitigate some of the damage. And many are already doing a lot.

We are recycling most of our waste. Unfortunately, most of this is being shipped to China. They realize its value and are no doubt taking advantage of our collective lack of initiative. But slowly we are getting better. I note that here in Chico there is a place producing biodiesel from recycled vegetable oil. They get a steady supply from restaurants all over Chico. Now, that's encouraging, isn't it? Maybe American ingenuity is not dead.

There are ads on the radio saying to bring in old motor oil for recycling. They can clean it up and reuse it in cars. Old batteries and used paint need special attention so they don't poison the environment. These may be small steps but "a journey begins with one step."

Now most of us bring our own bags for groceries and other shopping. That saves from using plastic bags which will not burn or even decay for – well – they estimate hundreds of years. One day it may be proven but no one will remember the first part of the argument! They say that in the middle of our beautiful Pacific Ocean is a mass of trash the size of continental USA. A pig would be shamed.

For several years we drove small cars to save gas, as a gesture to being less hoggish on the road. Now I notice everyone drives big cars, often pick-ups. Moderate-sized are what we used to call big. Not more than one in 12 are small.

But then I hear that in big cities bicycles are making a comeback. Bike lanes are being considered for safety. In Chico, a nice flat town, bicycles are used often. They certainly have a light footprint. On the plus side there are electric cars, non-polluting and quiet. I have a neighbor with solar panels on her house and an electric car.

She charges the battery of her car using the power generated from her solar panels. She is totally off the grid! There must be many people like that.

Slowly we are, on a local basis, trying to counteract some of the harm done to our earth. These are a few things I have seen locally. Organic gardens, stores and farmers' markets will help all of us to eat better with more fruits and vegetables. Human health will increase if we do this seriously. For not only is the earth sickening from our thoughtless activities, but we are damaging our health too: the heavy air children breathe increases asthma. The obesity of so many is caused by poor nutrition and much inertia.

Perhaps we are waking up and forging ahead, person by person; we surely need to.

Beauty

An Irish poet I listened to on the radio was talking of beauty. He mentioned that in America beauty was confused with glamour. That may have been true if he spoke to only waitresses and hotel clerks on his visits. But I know that many of my friends do not think beauty is just skin-deep. They take great pleasure in a lovely sunset, in the full moon on a clear night, and in the grandeur of landscapes and seascapes, their beauty breathtaking. They have shared their joy in these with me.

There is beauty in the ballet dancers performing for us so perfectly it seems as though we are swept away by it all. We come away renewed, as if from a trip to a magical world. I have spoken to musicians who themselves were lifted into a higher state as they played either solo or with the whole orchestra. You can imagine the years of hard training it takes to be a pianist, singer or ballerina, let alone a truly great artist.

In everyday life one can have moments of perfect accord, of agreement in planning, a melding of ideas that feel almost unbelievable but enters like a cool breeze. It can be a movement of truth which reminds me of the old saying, "Beauty is truth, truth is beauty, that is all you know on earth, all you need to know."

So beauty is more than glamour and more than skin-deep. We have often seen a beautiful face giving us a pang of joy, only to be jarred when its owner speaks in a harsh, unfriendly voice. We want perfection all the way; it is natural in us, even though in our humanity we know our imperfections are many.

It is the universe that is beautiful…and we can look out at the natural scene and marvel at how it fits together and yet remains a great mystery.

Forest Ranch

My daughter drives me up to her house in the back of Forest Ranch. We take Route 32 up the hill, cut right off of 32 at the church. The road leads us on a winding route down the hill with hairpin curves and no vision ahead. The steep slope on the right side looks scary. After fifteen minutes of this we get to the bottom of the canyon and head up the other side. It is equally steep but somehow going uphill is not scary. Finally we level off onto a stretch of very bumpy dirt road, with the La Rocca winery on our left and a blueberry farm on our right. Then in a minute we are up a hill and into the driveway of my daughter's house. Her cat is happy we are there and presses around our legs in greeting.

I settle in for a few days. During the night I can hear the yapping of coyotes; occasionally a fox barks – it is a strange sound, flat, and almost ghostly. In the spring, a chorus of frogs lasts from dark to dawn; they live in a pond nearby. In the early morning birds sing. A woodpecker drums loudly on a dead stump. The call of the quail in the fields sounds like 'Chi-CA-go!' in a treble voice.

The cherry tree is getting ripe with fruit. A fox comes boldly up, climbs the tree, and feasts upon the fruit. I watch her from the living room window. It is a mother fox, because when her stomach shows, you can see that she has been nursing a brood of pups. So my daughter lets her eat her fill, and then she leaves with not even a thank you.

As the evening arrives and after sunset, I like to sit on the porch. As it gets dark, one by one, bats fly out of their hiding place in the eaves of the porch. Sometimes I sit and count them as they flap off into the night. The most I ever got to was 21, sometimes only 8 or 9. A strange but peaceful little activity.

Sometimes when the fruit is ripe in July or August a bear will come to feast. He is definitely not welcome. He tears down big branches and has wrecked a whole tree. The raccoons come for the plums and you can hear the rustling in the dark. So I settle in for a few days to enjoy these wild creatures.

Next week I will pick wild blackberries.

Reflections

Faith

The world is run on faith, it is like the skeleton on which we build all our edifices, humble or proud.

If we make a grass hut and live there, we do so in the belief that it will shelter us from the elements; it is home. We keep our important things there and our food.

We could say the same of our proudest skyscrapers. Our faith can be crushed after an earthquake. But then we build again because we must, and because we have faith and that keeps us from giving up.

There is religious faith where we believe in a certain arrangement of ideas. Any other arrangement except our own won't work, we say. All religions are a result of these beliefs. Our faith keeps us and them alive. We can make excuses for God after calamities because in our faith God can't be wrong. He is punishing us for some intransigence and we must do better.

Thus the world of humanity goes on, with the record of past

successes and failures. It would seem that we should have given up by now; this does not happen because we have faith. We just have to have good luck, good prayers and try harder.

Hope

'Hope' is the thing with feathers that perches in the soul. This line of poetry by Emily Dickenson is a lovely expression of one of our deepest and most useful feelings.

We are always hoping. For a nice day, for rain, for sunshine, for warm weather, for cool weather. There is no harm in hoping, and it is good for us. The weather will do as it will, and we know that, but we can't help but hope it will be as we need it.

See God in Each Other

Very simple statement — no word over five letters. But when you think how profound, it is quite another thing. I can do it fine with most people, but there are those dang others who jump into my way and stop my forward march. Those are the ones I have to see God in — the others are a piece of cake.

As I unravel our disagreements, it is clear to me that the other person causing me the problem is not such a bad sort after all. The only thing is, sometimes the mind gets ahead of the heart. In catching up and ironing out a few new difficulties my heart has to work harder.

God is the same in all of us. I try to remember this especially if I don't like someone very much. It gives me peace. Perhaps it offers one tiny step to ceasing making wars.

I will keep on trying to do this, See God in those pesky ones.

Love

I believe love spans our life. As a newborn we have it from our mother. In the end, as we die, we remember with love. We forgive and are forgiven and we are free to leave this world simply with love.

This is all a very happy and reassuring thought. If we practice virtues in between birth and death, we will have the tools to deal with obstacles and challenges, and then we can be more sure of dying in love, even if our lives may be full of hardships and endurance.

Joan was active to the end of her days, and died peacefully in her daughter's home on August 30th, 2020.

AFTERWORD—Return to Sorrento

Throughout our childhoods, our mother spoke of Sorrento and the farm, her brothers and sisters, and all the animals. As little children, we listened to her stories, imagining this place from long long ago where Pi the dog lived, where Mopsie baked pies, and where the family swam in a lake called Shuswap. As our Mum cooked supper or drove us to school, she told us about the time she fell off the horse or the garden she had kept, or her rabbits, or the one-room schoolhouse.

Mum never took us to see Sorrento, but in her final years she suggested that we sisters might go one day. It wasn't until after she died that the three of us banded together to make this all important trip. We were excited to step into the fairy tale world our mother had woven from all those stories.

The distances from the US were great, but finally we were able to make the trip in June 2023, Joan's three daughters and Greg, Kanaka's husband. Through the generous hospitality of the house's current residents, Shelly and Bo Larson, we were able to walk through the rooms that had been our mother's first home, the one she never forgot. We saw the sunny kitchen and the room where the shelves of leather bound books had been. Shelly gave us rhubarb that Mopsie had planted. We stewed it the way our Mum taught us, a dessert that she made every Spring throughout her life. We looked out across Lake Shuswap spread below and the mountains on the other side. The hay barn was still standing. We went up to Notch Hill where the train used to stop and into the hall where the dances had been. We gathered mementos from the banks of the lake and boated across its waters on a stormy day.

To stand in the place we had only been able to imagine for so many decades was magical and deeply moving. As children, we had never realized how magnificent the land was, and still is.

It was hard to leave, but we sensed that our visit had completed a circle. We'd brought our mother back to the place where she most belonged. Lake Shuswap seemed happy to welcome her home.

Joan Vernon Szabo was born at home in Sorrento, British Columbia on May 2, 1924, the fourth child of Augusta and Herman Vernon, the first to be born in Canada. Until she was 18 she lived on the family farm, a short walk from Lake Shuswap. After graduating from the University of British Columbia she worked in microbiology labs across Canada, and then in New Haven, Connecticut. There she met and married Miklos, a Hungarian graduate student attending Yale University. With their three daughters they lived in the Eastern United States and England, while her last decade was spent in California. Though she travelled far in her 96 years, the natural setting of her childhood and all she had experienced there never faded from her mind. In the last few years of her life Joan began to write, mostly of those early years on the farm, but also recording some of her thoughts and hard-won insights about the ups and downs of life.

www.ingramcontent.com/pod-product-compliance
Lightning Source LLC
Chambersburg PA
CBHW051550010526
44118CB00022B/2650